BRAINFOOD

POEMS BY ROBERT SALMON

BRAINFOOD

POEMS BY ROBERT SALMON

MEREO
Cirencester

Mereo Books

1A The Wool Market Dyer Street Cirencester Gloucestershire GL7 2PR
An imprint of Memoirs Publishing www.mereobooks.com

BRAIN FOOD: 978-1-86151-572-8

First published in Great Britain in 2015
by Mereo Books, an imprint of Memoirs Publishing

Copyright ©2015

Robert Salmon has asserted his right under the Copyright Designs and Patents Act 1988 to be identified as the author of this work.

This book is a work of fiction and except in the case of historical fact any resemblance to actual persons living or dead is purely coincidental.

A CIP catalogue record for this book is available from the British Library.

This book is sold subject to the condition that it shall not by way of trade or otherwise be lent, resold, hired out or otherwise circulated without the publisher's prior consent in any form of binding or cover, other than that in which it is published and without a similar condition, including this condition being imposed on the subsequent purchaser.

The address for Memoirs Publishing Group Limited can be found at
www.memoirspublishing.com

The Memoirs Publishing Group Ltd Reg. No. 7834348

The Memoirs Publishing Group supports both The Forest Stewardship Council® (FSC®) and the PEFC® leading international forest-certification organisations. Our books carrying both the FSC label and the PEFC® and are printed on FSC®-certified paper. FSC® is the only forest-certification scheme supported by the leading environmental organisations including Greenpeace. Our paper procurement policy can be found at www.memoirspublishing.com/environment

Typeset in 11/17pt Ariel
by Wiltshire Associates Publisher Services Ltd. Printed and bound in Great Britain by Printondemand-Worldwide, Peterborough PE2 6XD

ACKNOWLEDGEMENT

First I must thank God for making this possible, for without him nothing is possible. Then I must raise my hat to this wonderful woman God sent to make this possible, Frances Carter. Without her this would not have been possible. I also thank my family and friends for their encouragement.

Thank God for life.

Robert Salmon

CONTENTS

VOLUME 1

DON'T GIVE UP	P.1
EDUCATION	P.2
FIGHT FOR SUCCESS	P.2
GOOD PARENT	P.3
INFLUENCE	P.4
MY SEED	P.5
OBEDIENCE	P.6
OPPORTUNITY	P.7
ROAD TO SUCCESS	P.7
SCHOOL DAYZ	P.8
STRIVE	P.9
THE EARLY YEARS	P.10
UNRULY PICKNEY	P.11
WISE UP	P.12

VOLUME 2

ANSWER TO WHY	P.13
ATTENTION	P.14
CHECK YOURSELF	P.15
CLEAN UP YOURSELF	P.16
DEFENCE	P.17
GHETTO LIFE	P.17
GOOD OVER EVIL	P.18
IDENTITY	P.19
LAWLESS LIFE	P.20
NO DRUGS	P.21
NUH RIGHT	P.22
OPPORTUNIST	P.23
PATIENCE	P.24
POLITICS	P.25
SEARCH FOR UNITY	P.26
TAKE HEED	P.27
TAKING ADVANTAGE	P.28
THOUGHTS	P.29
WAR AND PEACE	P.30
WHO CARES	P.31
WISE AND FOOL 2	P.32

VOLUME 3

ANY SIZE	P.33
BE YOURSELF	P.34
CONSCIOUS WOMAN	P.35
FEEDING TREE	P.36
FORGETFUL	P.36
FRIEND ENEMY	P.37
FRIENDSHIP FAIL	P.38
FRUSTRATION	P.39
HEARSAY	P.40
HONESTY IS THE BEST POLICY	P.41
JUST LIKE ME	P.42
KARMA	P.43
LIVE A CLEAN LIFE	P.44
NEW INVENTION	P.45
PROGRESS	P.46
RELATIONSHIP	P.47
TELEPHONE TALK	P.48
THE BULLY	P.49
TRUE LOVE	P.50
WEDDING VOWS	P.51
WISE AND FOOL	P.52

VOLUME 1

DON'T GIVE UP

Boast not because of your achievement, give thanks instead
Weep not because you have failed
Pick yourself up and try again
Life does not always come with success and joy
Life sometimes come with failure and sorrow
But always remember that today can lead you into a bright tomorrow
At the beginning of a tunnel there is light
At the end of a tunnel there is light
Success and failure are like light and darkness
If you in the light happy are you
If you in the dark continue going through
There is one thing you must understand
Things can change in a split second
Just live up, don't give up.

Education

While you are growing learn all you can
To make yourself a progressive man or woman
Don't feel proud because you are represented by an institution
Feel proud because you represent an institution.
Intelligence is not judged by what you have been taught
Intelligence is judged by what you have learnt.
Don't be satisfied with 100% progress
Doing your best is never good enough
Life can be rough even for the educated
Whatever you do, make sure you are dedicated
Aim high to the best of your ability
Save yourself from a degrading calamity.

Fight for success

Your plan for success
Will be put to the test
Setbacks and criticism you will face
Don't give up the race
When you think you are not on the go
Perseverance you must show
Even when things are going wrong
Hold on to your baton and be strong
Every stone thrown at you

Use it to pave your way through
When you finally reach your target
There will be nothing to regret
Blood sweat and tears
Carry on without fears
You are a success
You are truly blessed.

GOOD PARENT

Parent, teach your children to be a parent
That when you become grandparent
You don't have to be your grandchildren's parent
Show your children love and affection
Even when they are big men and women
That when they become parent they will pass it on
For some will not understand the role their parents play
Until they too play the role of a parent.
What is the meaning of the word parent?
Parent does not mean being a mother or a father
Parent means a mother and a father who love and care for their children.

INFLUENCE

Aged sixteen you a sleep out, not coming home
The street you a roam
Chatting up every girl you meet in the street
Make you feeling sweet
Everything that you want you parent give to you
Yet in a the house you nuh see nothing to do
Me know phases in life you have to pass through
You just have to be careful of the things that you do
The streets I know you have to use every day
But make sure you are on the right of way
You have a little saying called follow fashion
It good and bad, you must choose the right one
You in the street having a good time
Don't let violence walk in and mess up your mind
Walk away from trouble is the right thing to do
Going to prison is nothing good for you
Don't worry about friends calling you a chicken
For when you in prison them in KFC finger lickin'
And worse than that, you little girlfriend
Might just end up with you best friend
The street is filled with the have and have not
Please be content with whatever you got
Work hard to achieve what you don't
For someone else's thing try not to give an account.

MY SEED

Like a seed I was planted
Within walls I was embedded
Swimming in deep water
Searching for my shadow
To make my true reflection
For my perfection
I was on the verge of giving up
When I finally ignited with me
Because this was meant to be
Praises be to the father almighty
I did not have the power of thought
To know this was where prison sentence start
Nine months hard labour in darkness
My only visitor comes spraying water over my body
And then was gone like nobody.
Nevertheless I had regular visits
Time passes like the wind
My release date was announced
Soon I will be set free
No longer in captivity
Without warning the day arrived
I was pushed out with force
Smelling my first breath of fresh air
Before I had time to open my eyes
To behold the light

I listened to the whisper of a little voice
Saying you are my greatest miracle
This day you are bless bless blessed.

OBEDIENCE

It is indeed very nice to see
The young showing respect to the elderly
Likewise it's a pleasure to know
The elders appreciate the respect they show
When you young and have no respect for the old
Will you want respect from the young when you are old?
Can't say you haven't been warned
The good shown today will guide you tomorrow
Disrespect to you father is no glory to you
So be careful of the things you say and do
If the old provoke you to wrath
A fight you should never start
Just pour out a cup of love in his path
And if he continues to flip
Pour another cup till he start to slip
Then you pour another cup that he take a grip
Surely your name will be called among the peacemakers
And keep you far away from the undertakers
Honour the mother and father of the earth
That you live to see what life is worth.

Opportunity

What a golden opportunity you have and don't know
It in a you house and you a search out a door
Just take a good look inside you house
Check on you laptop you don't need a mouse
Tap in the words 'opportunity search'
Save it under my goal in life
Did you know that inside of you
You find everything you say and do?
But guess what, you live to say what you want
And do what you say
Never you think that you can't
You can always achieve what you want.

Road to Success

Why do you look so sad and forsaken
Are you not satisfied with the road you taken?
Do you think you have not achieved what you should?
Is it that you have not achieved what you could?
Don't say you are a failure and sit down and cry
You are a failure because you fail to try
Don't demean yourself because of your misfortune
You are very fortunate your life is still in tune
Never think it's too late to walk through an open gate

The way is clear, don't stand in your own way
The game is on, join the play
Today is your day, take up the baton of success
Don't stop going try your best
And when you reach your goal
Count a blessing and be bold
Keep going, you still have the potential
To take the highest seat amongst the influential
Aim high to the best of your ability
Your future is for real, not a probability.

SCHOOL DAYZ

When I was a youth going to school
Me use to sit a back bench acting like a fool
Now I am a man I understand
The importance of education
Went for a interview the other day
First thing the woman ask for is my resume
Me say lady to work in the office I can't
The packing job me really want
She say I am sorry young man
But we still need to see some qualification
Me get vex and start to fuss
She say same ting, him not ambitious
I left the office with this in mind

Not to let my children waste their time
Education is worth more than silver and gold
Staying with you until you are old
Silver and gold will vanish away
But a good education is there to stay.

STRIVE

Who are you to judge?
Put aside envy and grudge
Don't hate a brother for what he possess
Shake yourself up, join the line of success
Laziness is a serious crime
Forcing potential people to waste their time
Blessings are there for one and all
Just answer when the father call
Miss your chance of achievement
Grab another and be content
On earth there is enough to make us happy
Be a man, not a carbon copy.

THE EARLY YEARS

When you are young and carefree
Think about when you grow up what you want to be
Do not waste the time of your youth
Becoming a big tree that bear no fruit
Plant a seed when you young, nurture it as you grow
So when you get older you will reap from the seed you sow.
Children that set their goals
Will reach them before they grow old
Parent, help to educate your children
This will help to make you proud in the end
The home is where learning begin
Help to make them and don't give in
Though sometimes they are reluctant and stubborn
Don't stop pushing them to carry on
Children, there might be other keys to success
Don't forget, education is the best
Now is the time to decide your mind
The cassette of life you cannot rewind.

UNRULY PICKNEY

What a situation upon the land
We no have no little one
Everyone a big man and woman
Them reach age ten
You can't talk to them again
Buy them clothes find them food
In you house them have attitude
One thing me want them to know
Who bring them here and help them grow?
To obey is better than sacrifice
Disrespect to your parent is not the right choice
For when it is time to pay the price
Then you going to want you parent advice.
But me sorry, it's gonna be too late
Father god already decide you fate.

WISE UP

Why do I have to say the same thing
Again and again
Adding more stress to the brain
Feeding the heart with pain?
Still I'm talking in vain
Can't the young mind
Sit back and just unwind
Listen to the words of the wise
To open the eyes
Broaden your vision
To fulfil a successful mission?
Are you too young to understand
You are doing something wrong?
Don't hide from the council of wisdom
To end up losing your freedom
Put aside the lust for success
Work your way to progress
It's better to walk out of poverty
Than to run after riches.

VOLUME 2

ANSWER TO WHY

Sit and wait for nothing, hoping for something
Exploring my mind searching to find the truth
The lie, the answer to the question why
Why does the baby cry when they want nothing?
Why does the big people lie when they want something?
Why does the poor apologise even though he is innocent?
Why does the rich add reproach when he is guilty?
Why do parents neglect their children?
Why do children neglect their parents?
Why food spoiling and people dying for hunger?
Why sweeping the streets and the house full of litter?
Why life is so sweet and sometimes taste so bitter?
Can somebody tell me why there is no answer to why?

ATTENTION

This is a message to all youth man
Black white and Indian
Full bred, half bred, any bred
Wake up, pull up you pants
Stop from living in ignorance
Life is a long road paved with opportunity
Joining community to community
Grab yours now that you are strong
You don't have to do wrong to be a man
Yes it may seem attractive and sweet
Meeting and greeting the thugs in the street
But what about life in a prison cell
Causing loved ones a traumatic hell?
If you are on life's road doing wrong
Stop now and change direction
Be an example for your peers
Educate the young, show them you care
Your life is important not only to you
But also for those who may emulate you.

CHECK YOURSELF

Say no more, say no more
I have heard what you said
I will pick myself up, brush myself off
No longer will I give onlookers a laugh
No longer will I be a drag on the community
Begging bread and asking for pity
No longer will I pick up what you have thrown away
To make my meal for the day
Who sent me to roam the streets of poverty?
Nobody but me
Who can turn my life around?
Nobody but me
Today I have turned over a new page
To progress from stage to stage
As my life goes on
I will strive to be a better man.

CLEAN UP YOURSELF

Please my brother please my brother
Don't hate me for the strong thought of my weakness
It's bothering me, I got to get it off my chest
Can't you see what drugs doing to society?
Do you have to be a part of this community?
What about the woman in pregnancy
And the one nursing a young baby?
What about the young children exposed to drugs
Because parent can't control their habit
Would you do this to your own children?
No, that what you say?
Well what you don't want for yourself
Don't give it to others
Please my brothers and sisters, don't sell drugs
Don't take drugs
You are hurting others
While you hurting yourself.

DEFENCE

I am fighting a war in my brain
The battle is so intense
Attack coming from every angle
They are fighting to destroy my temple
They attack me with war, I fight back with peace
They attack me with hate, I fight back with love
They attack me with separation,
I fight back with togetherness
They attack me with segregation,
I fight back with oneness
They attack me with false accusation,
I fight back with true confession
They attack me with hands filled with reward,
I fight back with a heart filled with refusal
They are fighting in vain
They cannot mess up my brain my brain my brain.

GHETTO LIFE

Life in the ghetto can be better
Life in the ghetto could be worse
Life in the ghetto can be a blessing
Life in the ghetto could be a curse
Think of the ghetto children

Don't grow them like lions in a den
Teach them to realise
They too can be humble and wise
Hey! You, miss Beverly Hill
What happen to your sister Wareka Hill?
And you, miss Cherry Garden
Remember your brother Arnette Garden?
Life in the ghetto is what you make it
Opportunity come, you got to take it
Elevate yourself to the highest point
Still don't forget your ghetto joint
When you are blessed in health and wealth
Always remember how ghetto life felt.

GOOD OVER EVIL

Who are you to dig my pit?
You full of s***
You shall fall in it
You rise up against me without reason
Forgetting that I am a man of all season
You secretly plan my hurt
Not knowing that I am bless from birth
You slander me with words of hate
Hoping that I would lose my faith
Wicked men is time you see

No evil can come near me
Now you know you can't hurt this man
Seek forgiveness while you can
I am the I am that I am
Who are you?
I am a miracle of the nation
Perform by the god of creation
Who are you?
I am Daniel closing the jaws of the hungry lions
Who are you?
I am Shadrach, Meshek and Abednigo
Walking out the fire without getting burn
Who are you?
I am Joseph dragged from the well
Who are you?
I am your brother Abel sending your soul to hell
Who are you?

IDENTITY

Identify yourself, show your rarity
Persist in being proud and hearty
Show love and affection towards humanity
Put aside the lust for gold and vanity
What is the difference between the rich and the poor?
Sickness, death and pain knock on everyone's door
The most powerful man was once a baby

So were you and also me
From the beginning it was meant to be
That people should be treated equally
Some might be lawyers, some might be doctors
Doesn't matter who you are, we are all human characters
Listen to your heartbeat and weigh your brain
You don't need an umbrella to walk in the rain
Your God-given power is so strong
Use it wisely and you can't go wrong.

LAWLESS LIFE

Children a cry parent a ball
Guns and bayonet pointing over the wall
Shoot out shoot out
One lady a shout
Get up an run a father call out to his son
You no hear say police a come
Get up out a de blasted bed
You no know say you wanted
Guns blazing shots echoing
Police in full riot gear
Shooting like they don't care
Rawtid one police get shot mi nuh know if him dead
But me see the helmet fly off him head
Waay waay dem kill Johnny

And dem box down him granny
Bwoy dem police yah serious today
Mek mi try get out dem way
Officer a work mi a go sah
Me is a teacher
You could be a preacher
Get on the floor before you skull get bore
Unuh shot one of my squaddie
Now me nuh respect nobody
Weh bad boy Trevor
Is him we come for
If we don't kill him today
Someone else will have to pay
Lord protect me I pray
Don't let Babylon blow me away

NO DRUGS

To the young, to the old, to the middle-aged I am appealing
Please stop the drugs using and the drugs dealing
Are we to blind to see
Drugs is destroying our society?
I am so vex and ashamed of this silly game
But the perpetrators don't want to take the blame
What joy and satisfaction it bring
To be in the street doing your thing?

Not thinking of the pain and sorrows it cause
When you are sleeping behind bars
Sharing the unpleasant luxury of a small cell
Your mate use the toilet you can't stand the smell
Keys dangling doors slamming
You don't have no choice of the food you nyaming
It is not a shame and disgrace
To throw away dirty works and clean up the place
Do society a big favour
You can be another life saver.

NUH RIGHT

Something nuh right at all
Something nuh right
Look how the people them a fuss and fight
Dem fighting for peace
And want the fighting to cease
Something nuh right
Them left from abroad
Come in a me yard
Kill me mother me father
Me sister and brother
Tell me that nuh hot
You tell me to forget about that
Something nuh right

You in a corner like a rat
Hiding from a cat
Fighters out there a dodge gun shot
You big idiot storm coming go fight that
Hurricane a come go stop that too
Natural disasters you don't know what to do

OPPORTUNIST

When there is plenty food on your table
There are chairs everywhere
Soon as the table is empty
All the chairs disappear
It's good to live happy with family and friends
But this only rarely happens
If you are not in a position to give
No one appreciates the life you live
Good friends are rare very hard to find
Don't search for one, you are wasting time
Treat friends like today
Coming then going away
Life without friends is miserable and sad
But it's worse when a friend treat you bad
Be surprise to find a good friend
But don't be surprise when the friendship ends
Care to know why friendship come to an end
Check the last three letters in the word friend.

Patience

I can't stay awake or go to sleep
My cool I am fighting hard to keep
The humble and fragile to be fierce and agile
Sometimes I am on the edge of fury and explosion
But the looks and thoughts of my children
Overcome my emotion
Why was I chosen to suffer this pain of endurance
That I am looked at as weak and defenceless?
What a day it will be when the peacemaker go to war
And the warriors can't be at peace
Begging for the war to cease
When dead lions will be no match for live sheep
Then the humble shall rise and the wicked put to sleep
Father bless me and let it be
That the words hidden in my heart
Not to sin against thee.

POLITICS

Twelve o'clock in the night, can't sleep so I start to write
The thoughts that rush to my brain
The thought of countries fighting in vain
Telling lies for reason to invade
Then making apologies for mistakes they made
Killing the young old and innocent
Giving them no time to even repent
The thoughts that rush to my head
Make me refuse to go to bed
The killing of the innocent fill my heart with discontent
Then come the uncontested political speeches
Giving reason and cover for their breaches
Saying they using war to make peace
Never heard of that, must be some brand new release.

Search for Unity

Where is the love light that used to shine
When mine could be yours and yours could be mine?
Where is joy and peace that live in the community?
There is no more of such love and unity
Hatred and grudge has taken control
Causing war and destruction of the soul
When will it end, why did it even start?
In the net of corruption mankind has been caught
Some seem to enjoy living this filthy way
Others wish it would stop this very day
Is mankind too blind to see
That sickness pain and death carries no partiality?
The man you wish to fall down
Might watch you moulded up in the ground
The spirit of love will decide your fate
Try not to live in the spirit of hate.

TAKE HEED

Judge not that he be judged
Grudge not that he be grudged
Envy not that he be envied
Hate not that he be hated
Show love that he be loved
Be caring that he be cared for
Be merciful that he can obtain mercy
Be honest so that he be treated honestly
Be at peace with your enemy
Though he is not a friend
Be wary of a friend
Thou he is not an enemy
It is better for an enemy to become a friend
Than a friend to become an enemy
Yet neither is good, both are like fire in the bosom.

TAKING ADVANTAGE

How long how long will I have to wait
For a little food to be placed on my plate?
Do I have to set my plate under your table
To catch the crumbs that fall from your plate?
Do I have to stand outside your gate
Begging for the refuse you going to throw away
For you to tell me sorry come back another day?
The rich and powerful feed the poor like birds
Throw them their bits without saying a word
You give me machete an file to cut your grass
You then examine it before you pay what you think it cost
I'm not going to live this derogatory way forever
No no I will never
I will no longer be a fool in the abundance of water
I have my family and folks to look after
The grass is green, I will feed my flock
Without fear of the power trying to hold me back
Down presser then you realise before you fall
That equality and justice stand for all.

THOUGHTS

Three o'clock in the morning
Day will soon be dawning
Sitting on my bed, should be sleeping instead
The day's activity I try to rewind
Searching for a little peace of mind
Trying to differentiate the arrogant from the ignorant
The phrases, the sentences, the speeches
The sense, the nonsense
The logic and what it teaches
Assertion, criticism, comparison
The facts and the fiction
The he say she say hear say
Know say and the prediction
The chattery the flattery the mockery tongue lashing
Comments and remarks that deserve a thrashing
But allow them to have their opinion
What them thinking
Mouth cut crossways to say anything.

WAR AND PEACE

What a situation upon the land
My gosh is what happen to man
The lion the tiger the leopard and cheetah
And other fierce animal were known man eater
Man turn it around and hunt them down
But now worse than them we face
Because man take them place
Man four-footed enemies could not attack as them please
Dem have to crouch on knees and hide in trees
Now your worst enemy could be your best friend
And you don't even know that him a pretend
What a situation upon the land
My gosh is what happen to man
Is there a way to stop this kind of living?
It is gone too far we can't do nothing
Mankind will never live comfortable
Until jah come sit at the table
Then war will derail
And peace prevail
To stop this situation upon the land.

WHO CARES

In the corner of my cubicle I wonder in meditation
Lo and behold I see a clear revelation
Man eating man like them eating bread
It was all chaos and laughter
No one weep for the dead
Men ordering the death of the unborn
Soon mother and child are gone
Look through the mirror of my eyes
You might be able to see
The dream that kept haunting me
The desire to see inequality and injustice uprooted
And oneness and justice implanted
In the corner of my cubicle I will sit and wait
Until destiny decides our fate.

WISE AND FOOL 2

The wise marvel at the success of the fool
The fool take no notice of the prosperity of the wise
The fool will take the seat of the wise
Likewise the wise will take the seat of the fool
It is honourable to see the fool living like the wise
But it's a curse to see the wise living like a fool.

VOLUME 3

ANY SIZE

My cousin went to a shoe shop
She bought a pair of size seven shoes
When she go home, shoes can't fit
Her sister ask what size shoe is that
She said size seven
Sister said so how you wear size eight
And buy size seven?
She said a because no number eight wasn't there.

BE YOURSELF

It make some happy to see you sad
You should be happy to know they are glad
How can the fall of another benefit you
Knowing that you can fall too?
What is it about me that bothers you?
Is it what I say or is it what I do?
Don't waste precious time trying to find
Peace and happiness in someone else's mind
Be content living with truth and commitment
Be wary of others' malicious intent
Life is not always a paved and smooth road
Sometimes it gets rocky and bumpy with a heavy load
Don't expect to be returned kindness for kindness
Or to be praised when you done your best
For every beat of the heart
Can be a change of the thought
Yet don't forget the answer is love
And only wisdom stands above.

CONSCIOUS WOMAN

You speaking to me thinking of another
Or talking to another thinking of me
Tell me the truth, let your heart set you free
How deep did you penetrate my soul
To make my heart feel so warm in the winter cold?
The strength of your love is in full control
Conquering a heart fearless and bold
You have a smile so bright
In the dark it shines a light
You should be hidden away from man
Your presence is too much temptation
You are a precious gem
A treasured collector's item.

FEEDING TREE

Poor me poor me the little feeding tree
Bearing fruits for the birds to feed
Birds come around when they are in need
Birds will perch for a little while
Soon they have to go before their business spoil
Poor me poor me the little feeding tree
The little feeding tree with many branches
On my smallest limb please do not take advantage
Birds don't have to eat too much before they go
Knowing that they can always come back tomorrow
Poor me poor me the little feeding tree
Even the patoo come out to feed on me
Those are the ones that come out at night you see
Thank you father bless this little feeding tree
So that the birds can rely on me
Poor me poor me the little feeding tree.

FORGETFUL

Me auntie call me phone
Me lose you number give me again
Me say then a me number this you call
She say me never sure me just
Want to make sure.

FRIEND ENEMY

Frienenemy frienenemy frienenemy
You have a friend face
But you nuh have a friend heart
You can't be friend to the end
If you a nuh friend from the start
You say you a me friend and a judge me
For what me have you a grudge me?
All these times you and me a spar
In a you heart me and you a war
Day by day me a try me best
Not to be fool by your friendliness
Me know long time say me friend a chat against me
Me just a find out him a plot against me
Me in me house a catch a dose
Me friend a look me wife under me nose
You have friend face but you don't have friend heart
You can't be a friend to the end
If you not a friend from the start.

Friendship Fail

The same door you open to a friend today
He might be closing to lock you out tomorrow
Careful what you say to him about a brother
He might make you an enemy to another
The arms of flesh will not fail
It's the heart of man that prevail
Don't chase down a friend walking away from you
Go the other way, that's the best thing to do
When friendship is being betrayed
Think for a while the part that you have played
Then forget about it, call it a loser's game
For that friendship will never be the same.

Frustration

I am happy it appears to be
All my sadness is inside of me
No one understands my pain and frustration
Fools insult my intelligence
And take for granted my patience
My blessings become my curse
My curse becomes my blessings
I quiver in the corner of my flat
Like a mouse hiding from a cat
I am love that is embraced by hate
Still I hug myself and wait
I hunger and thirst for real love
Given by the father above
Will someone please set me free
From this heartache, pain and misery?

Hearsay

Me say the hearsay business can't die out
Is what really happen to people mouth
The woman and her husband living in a war
Someone tell the man him hearsay she and man in a bar
She say she know is who as she walk in him left
But them going to learn to see and blind hear and deaf
Suppose dem did make the man beat me to death
Right now me don't know what a go happen yet
Because this argument can go very far
No man don't want hear him wife and man in a bar
You know sometimes me wish news carriers to die out
Or even them tongue cut out them mouth
But me going to tell my husband if him take me to court today
The judge a go run him out with him hearsay
Although is not lie them telling on me
Him too quick to believe wait till him see
But you know you have to forgive the news carrier man
Because someone tell me say him hearsay a same way him lose him woman.

HONESTY IS THE BEST POLICY

To speak the truth is the best thing to do
Sometimes its harsh, sometimes it hurts too
When you lie and it is found out
When it's time to tell the truth
You have to close your mouth
The truth is sometimes hard to reveal
Because you thought it might be a big deal
The truth might be an offence, but the blame is not on you
But to lie might need a confession
Which you might find hard to do
A truthful tongue adds perfection
But lying lips are an abomination
Before lying to others lie to yourself first okay?
If you don't find out you lying tell that lie straight away
I'm telling you the truth, this is a lie
I would rather die telling the truth
Than to live telling a lie
What a liard brute.

JUST LIKE ME

My best friend is just like me
Loving kind peaceful and carefree
My best friend and I share the same date of birth
Trodding the same place on earth
Like me my best friend never accept defeat
Prefer to stand up on his own feet
Seeing us together we are identical twins
Loving the same thing, sharing the same thing
My best friend and I are the same height, size and weight
We both share the same fate
Like me he thinks his children is him
For them he do any and everything
My best friend do what I do hear what I hear see what I see
My best friend is me.

KARMA

Today for you tomorrow for me
You alone can't be a community
Every day you huffing and puffing
At the end of this day you get nothing
To make me sad is your greatest delight
Doing it day and doing it night
Nothing you say and do can hurt me no more
Than you have hurt me before
Don't waste time fighting to win
Every champion end up losing
Hating me is a publicity
You tell it to everybody
My downfall is your greatest desire
My success sets your heart on fire
I love you as much as you love me
I hate you as much as you hate me.

LIVE A CLEAN LIFE

The war between good and evil raging warriors ageing
Yet the war has just begun
Children emulating eating and digesting
The good and bad thing
Continuing the fight for the wrong and right
Many not knowing what they fighting to achieve
Fighting because they have been deceived
So they end up in destruction
With no hope for resurrection
What will it take for us to realise
What we doing is not wise?
Destroying ourselves, our families our friends
When will this war come to an end?
No love no peace no hope for unity
Not even in the home, the first community
One thing I know for sure
The powers of the universe will open the door
And set his people free from this war between good and evil.

NEW INVENTION

Back in the days a country man went to Kingston
To look for his friend
The friend wasn't home so the wife cook him some food
Put it on the table with knife and fork table properly set
When him finish eat and she went to clear the table
The knife and fork was wrap up in the napkin unused
So a must be him finger him use
Anyway his friend come home and they had a reminiscing conversation
He then ask to use the toilet
When he finish he call out to his friend
Yow brethren a so unuh a live a town
You use the toilet press the lever and water come up fe wash you hand
The friend ask so you wash you hands
Him say how you mean man?
Think me a fool to that.

Progress

You are the reason I write this book
I want you to take a good look
Look into your life, the progress you could make
If you just reach out for a piece of the cake
Life is the greatest gift to man
Make the most of it while you can
Look towards the future not in the past
Stride to achieve your goal don't matter what the cost
You can do it, you can do it
Listen to that voice
You only have to make the right choice
Never say you can't and be too lazy to try
Always give a try, you will get by.

RELATIONSHIP

In a relationship the sea sometimes gets rough
You may even think you have had enough
But when the going gets rough and the rough gets going
If there is children on board remember they are still growing
When the sea is calm and you are in each other's arms
Make your pledge to stick together and whether the storm
In a relationship that is too smoothly sailing
You might find it hard to know if your engine is failing
When you are in a relationship you must realise
To get in another ship is not very wise
If you see another ship heading your way
Change your course and keep it at bay
In case you have to keep a lifeboat
Don't get in it while your ship is still afloat
But if your ship should wreck and you are still alive
Get in your boat and paddle to survive
This is a warning, take heed to it
No one person can go in two ship
If you try to do so, whether man or woman
You gonna end up in a ship collision.

TELEPHONE TALK

You know telephone has good and bad effect
Some calls you receive, some you reject
Telephone causes accidents and deaths
It can make you happy and make you fret
Breaking up of marriages and good relationship
Happens because of telephone gossip
A telephone call you should not ignore
That call could prevent you walking through death's door
A telephone call could warn you of a possible danger
Even if the call coming from a stranger
Telephone call can cause problem
Can also help to solve them
Tell you something telephone do to me
Walking down the road texting somebody
Head down not looking up
Straight in the lamp pole me buck up
Be careful how you use your telephone
You might be out a road and can't go home.

THE BULLY

Look big man the bully thing don't work
All it do is make you look like a jerk
When you meet the humble and weak
You loud up you beak like war you a seek
But when you see the bold and strong
You shake them hand even when them done you wrong
Hey youth man stop bully the little child
You don't know bully thing only last for a while
Make me tell you about one bully me know
Him bully this boy that school he didn't want to go
One evening he was walking with his friend
See the boy and bully him again
The little boy big brother was just in time to see
Went over to them and make him get on his knee
And say to his little brother sorry sir please be my friend
I won't ever bully you again
The bad thing is him lose his street cred
Him walking and holding down him head
The worst thing is him name was lorry
His friend start to call him lorry without trailer
What a failure.

TRUE LOVE

God bless the day I found you
It feels so nice being around you
Although you are not comprehensively insured
In my arms you are safe and secure
You still have to be aware
There are lots of body snatchers out there
So be careful of the game you play
Because the bird in hand might fly away
And the bird in the bush might not come to stay.
Therefore stick to the evil you already know
The good that starts today might turn evil tomorrow
Not everything that glitter is gold
Can't say you haven't been told.

BRAIN FOOD

WEDDING VOWS

A Rastaman was forced into marriage
On the day of the wedding
The Rasta took the pastor aside and said to him
Pastor when you reach the vow part
Remember to say till her death do us part
The woman don't like that, so she told the pastor to say
Till the manhood become dead do us part.

WISE AND FOOL

Fools judge you by your appearance
Wise judge you by your intelligence
Fools have eyes to see the outside
Wise have visions of the inside
Fools appreciate you for the way you attire
Wise appreciate you for the way you conduct yourself
A fool will insult you and know not
A fool will be insulted and know not
A fool can be easily taken for a ride
It is wise not to keep a fool by your side.

www.ingramcontent.com/pod-product-compliance
Lightning Source LLC
Chambersburg PA
CBHW061343040426
4244CB000111B/3070